This book belongs to

____

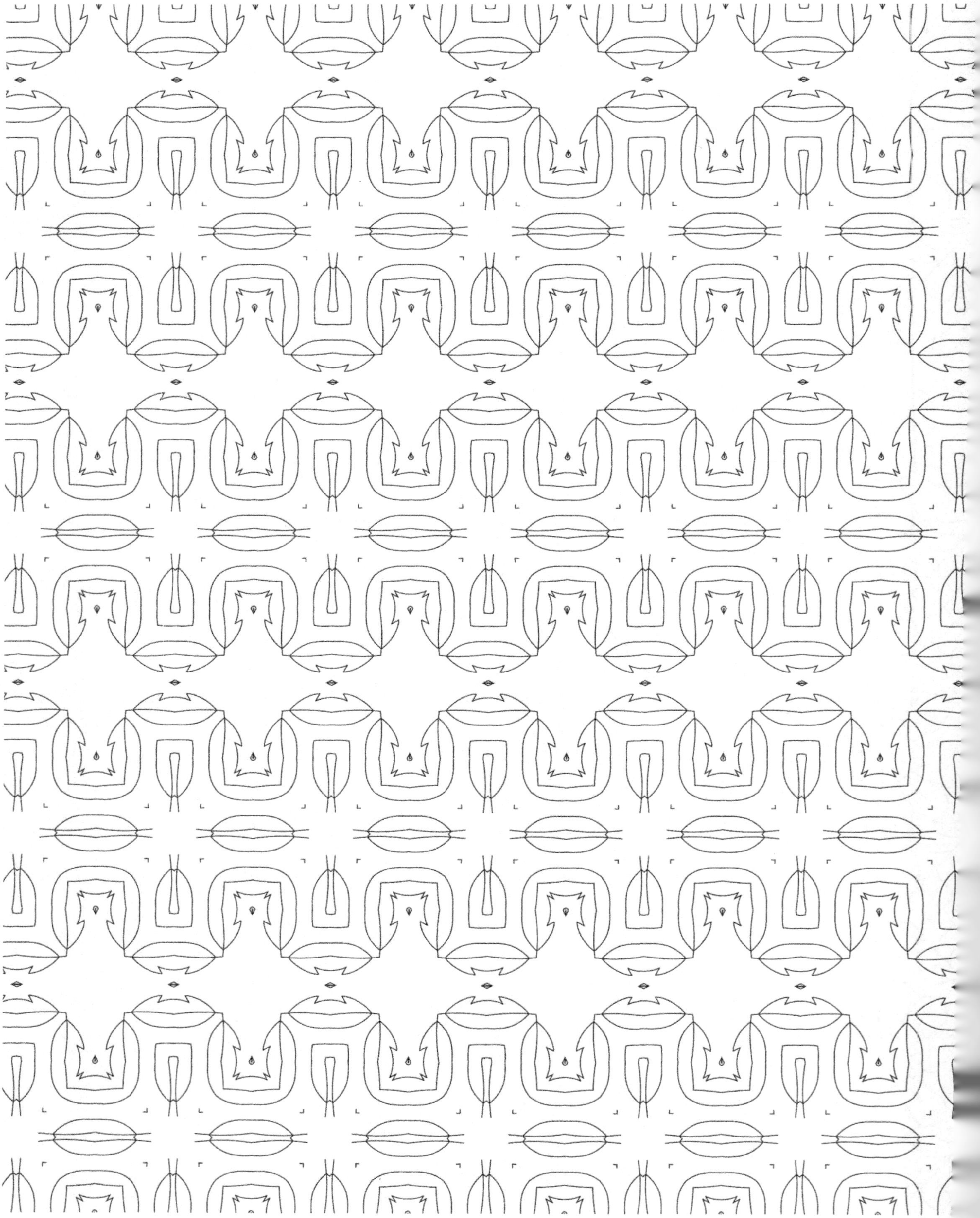

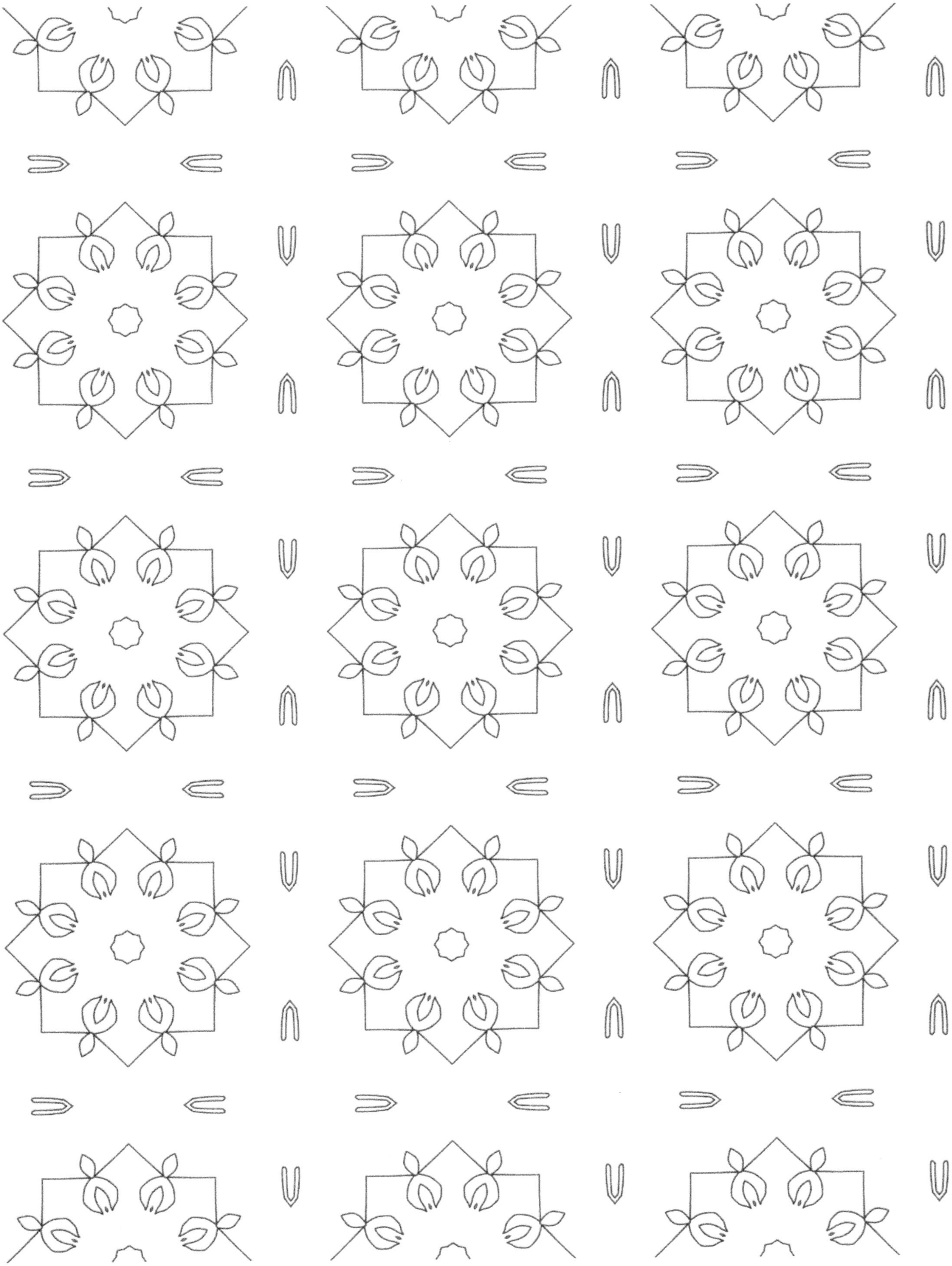

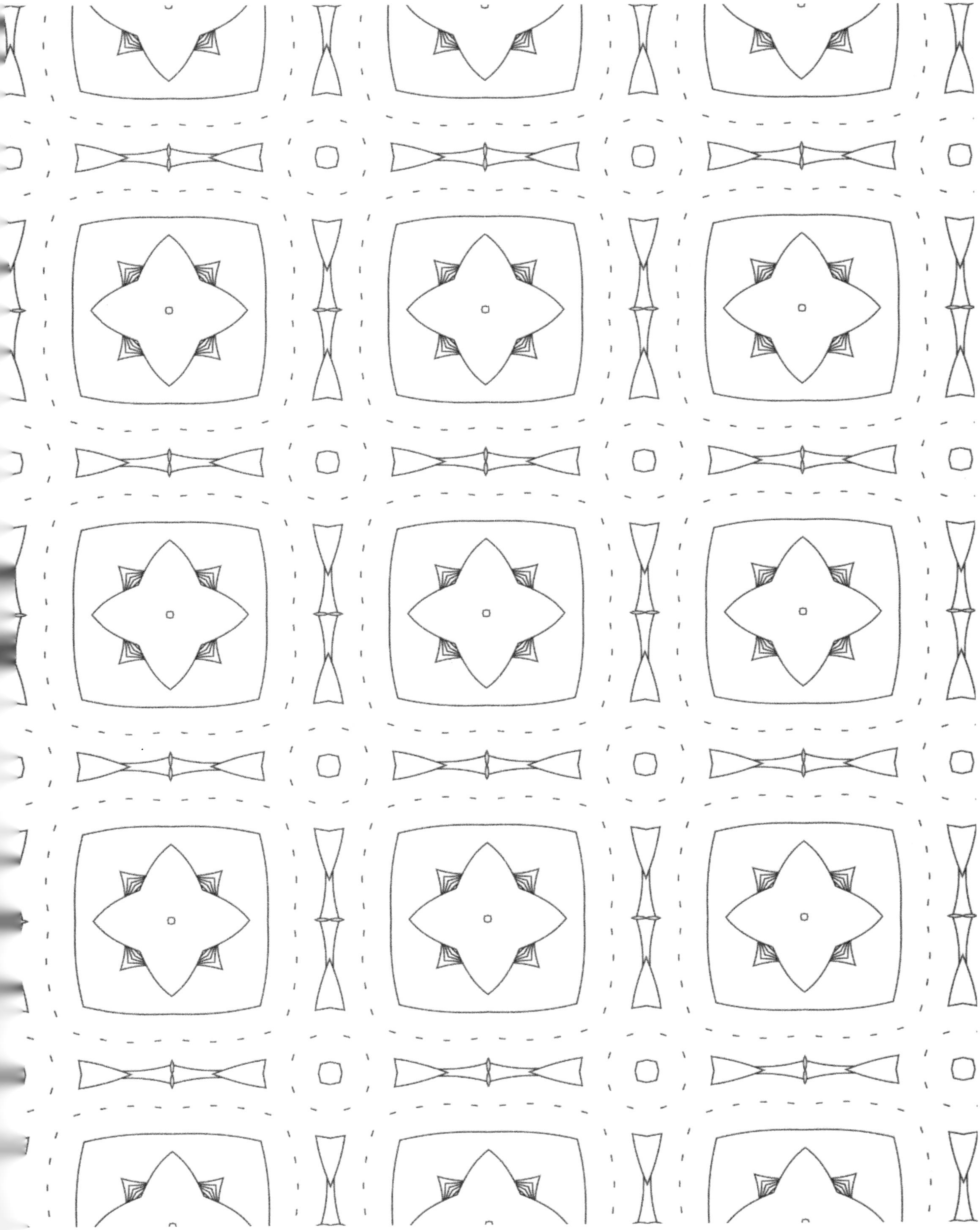

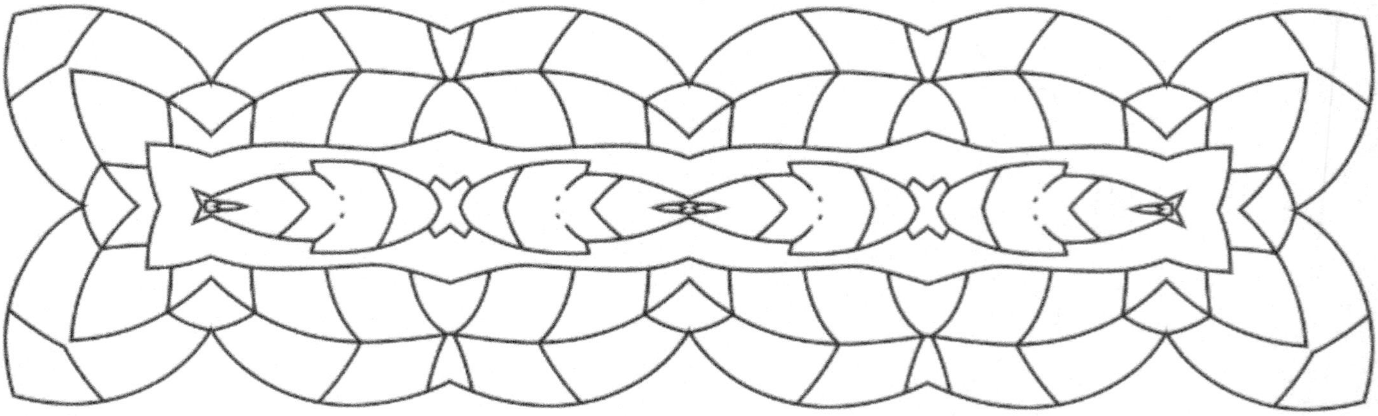
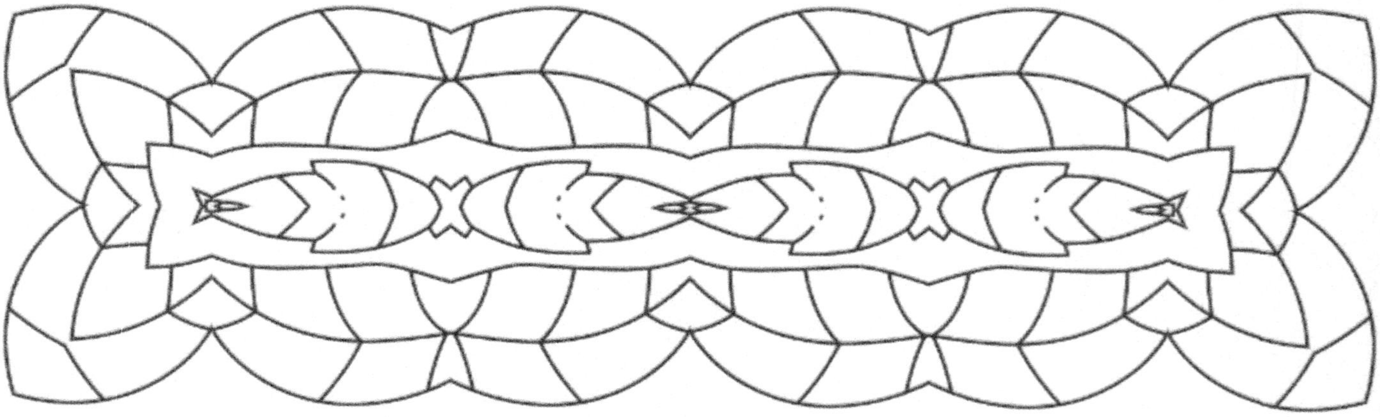
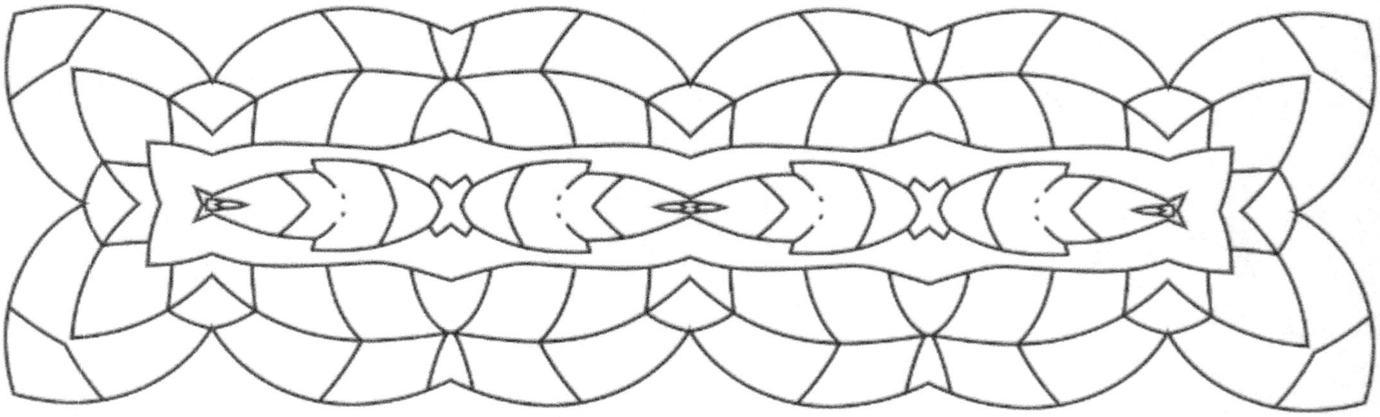
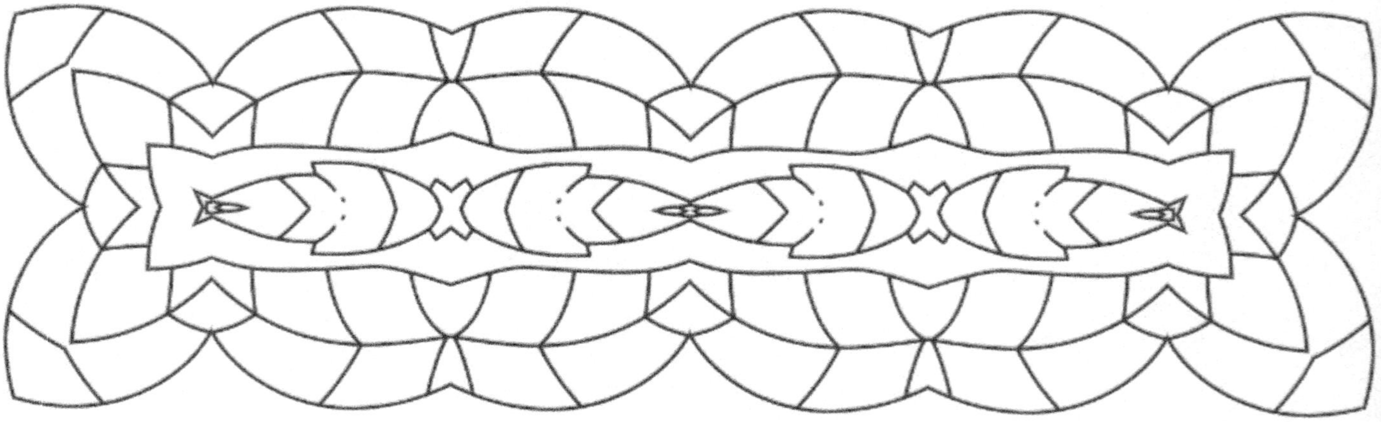

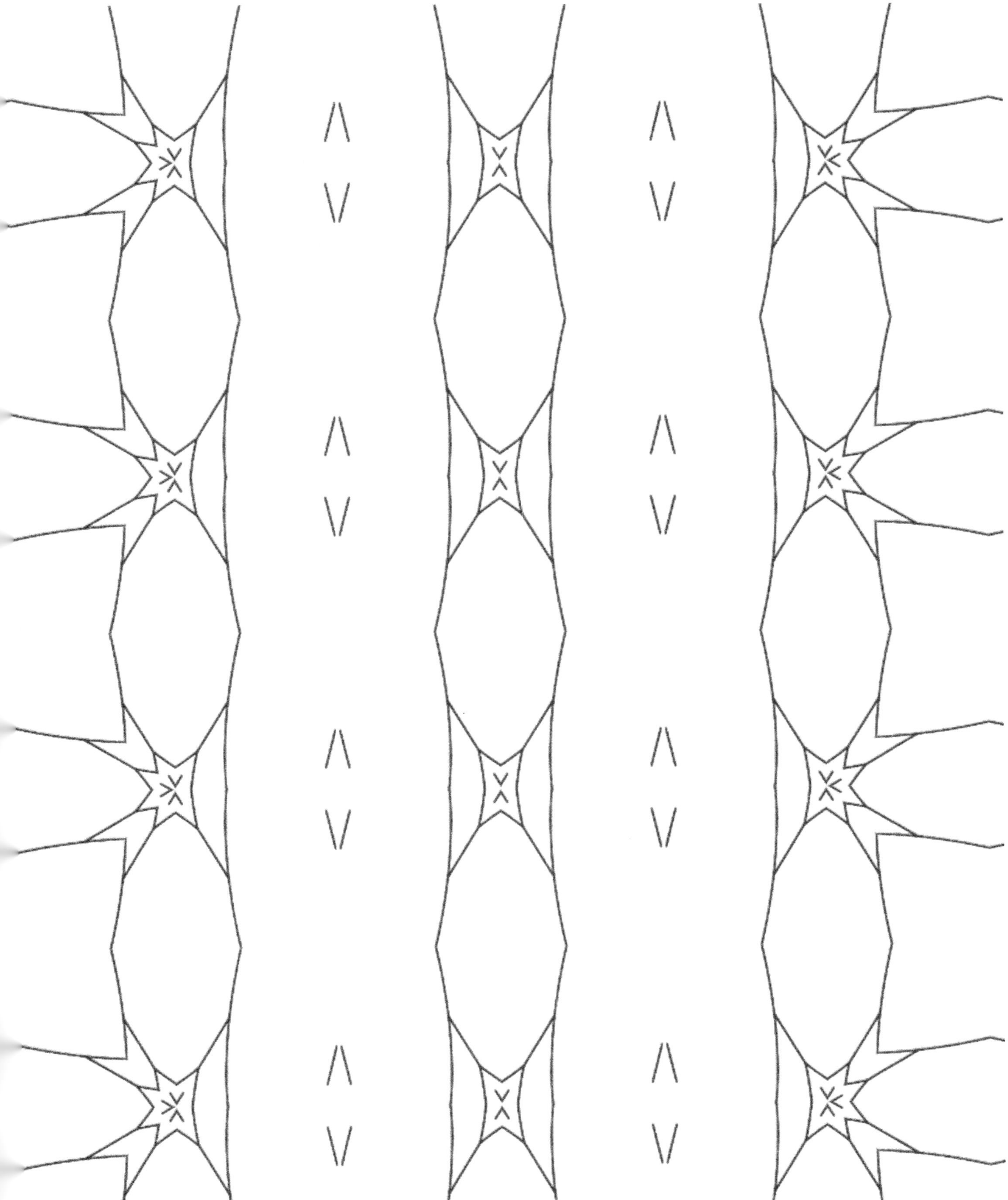

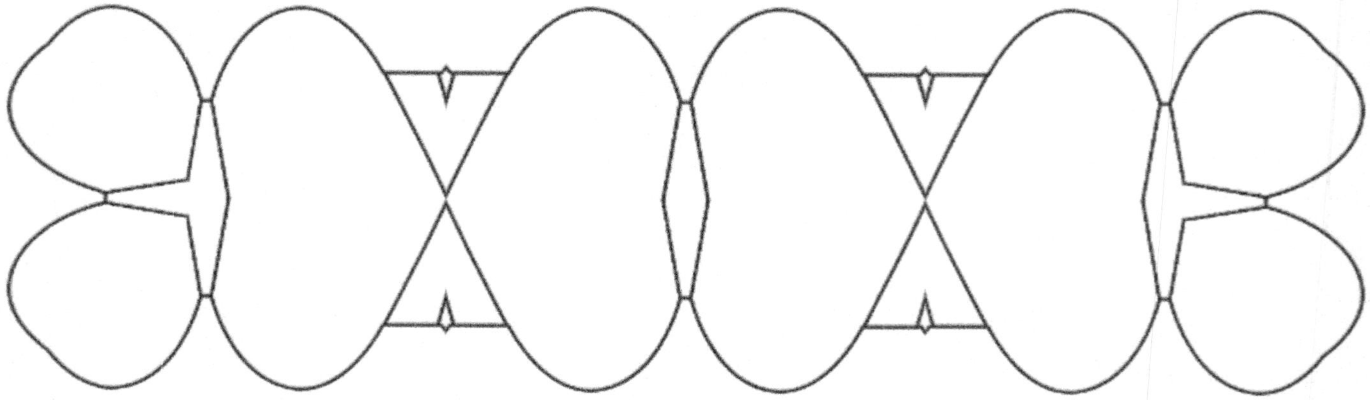
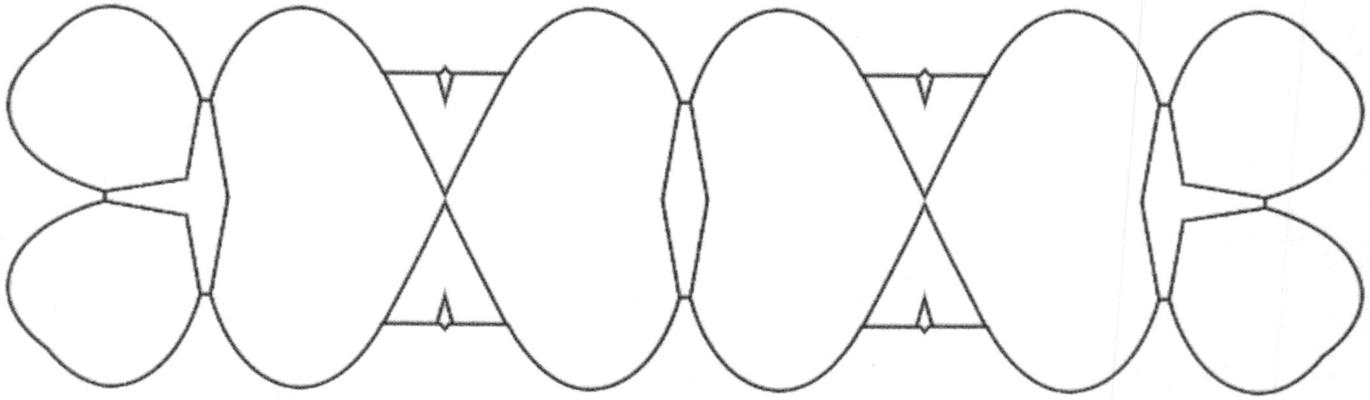
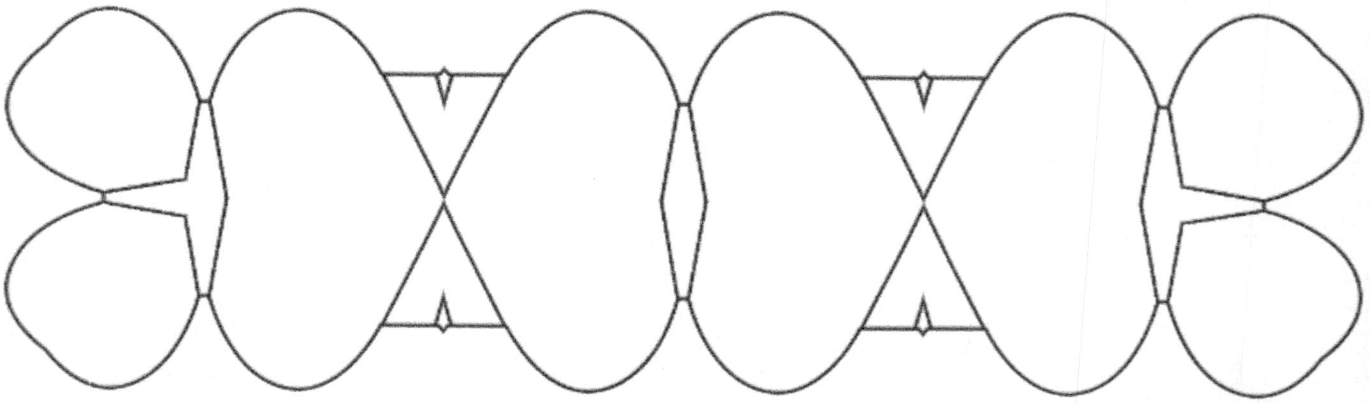
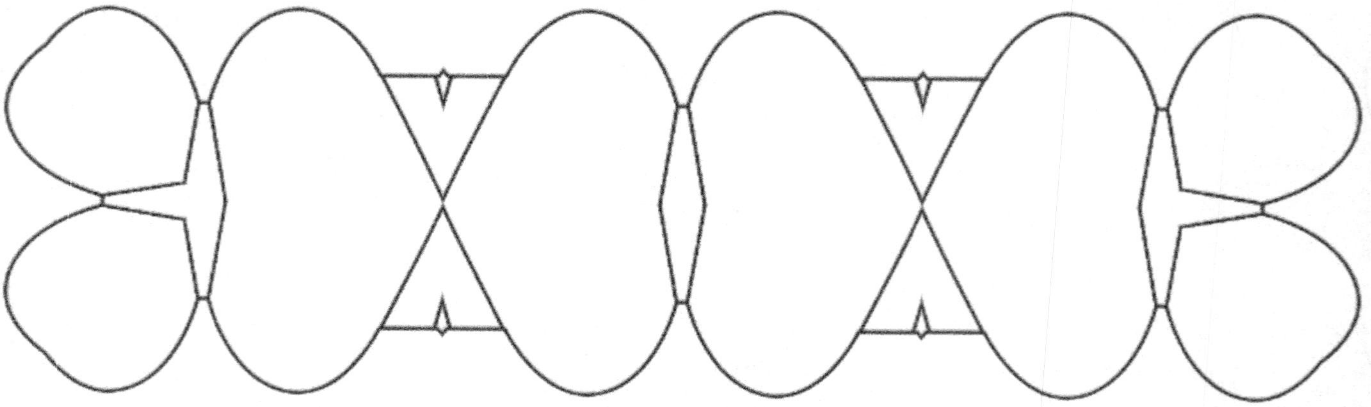

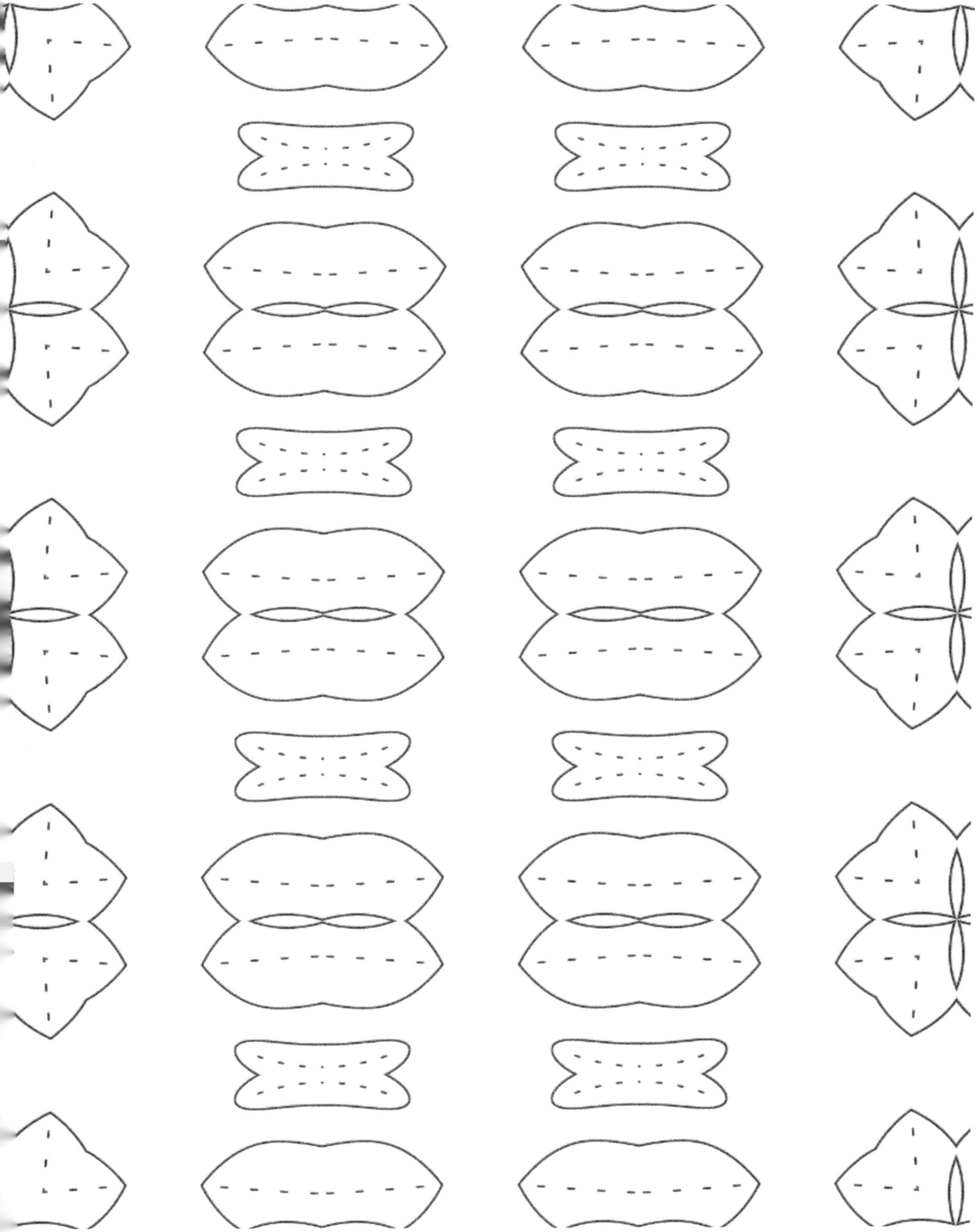

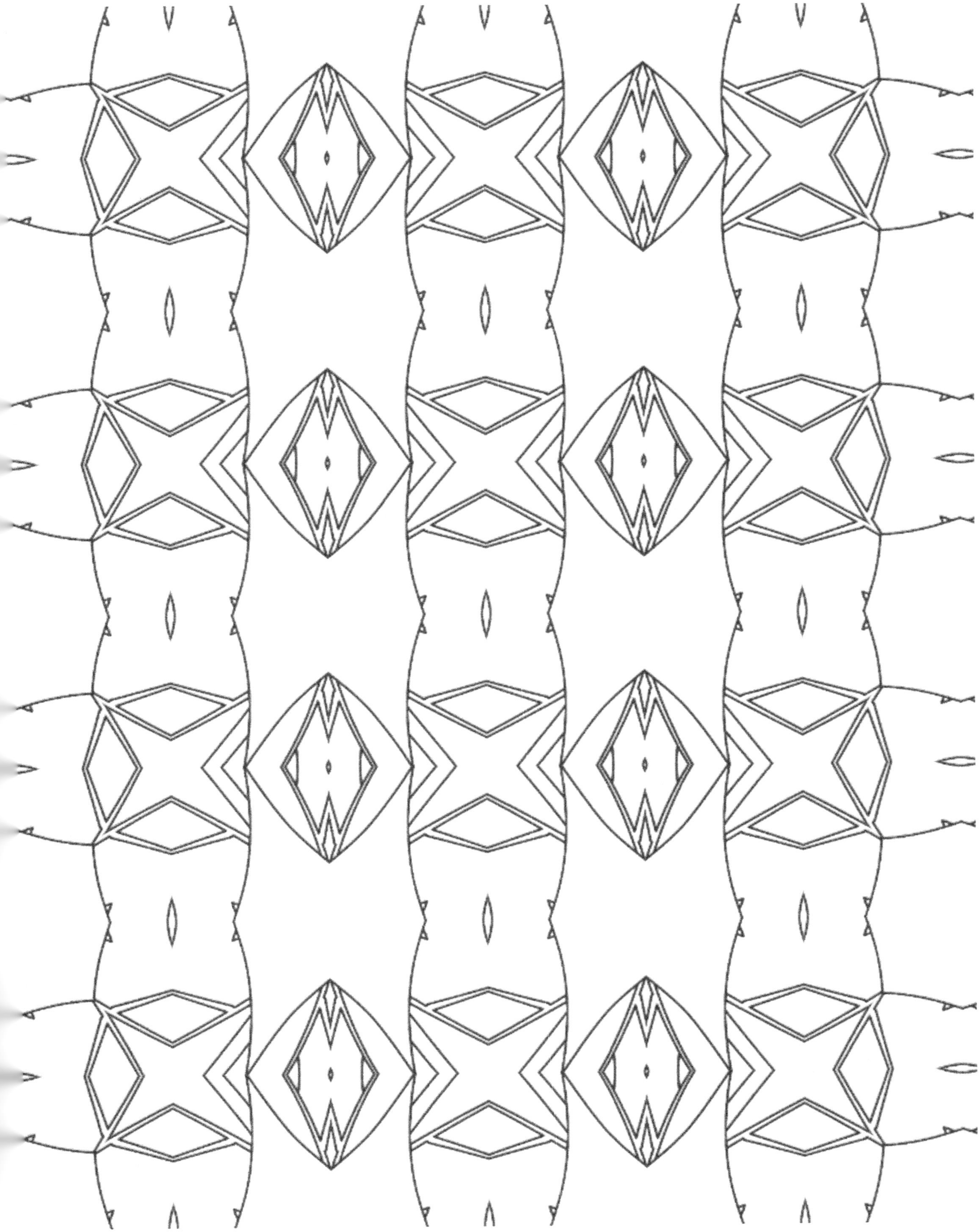

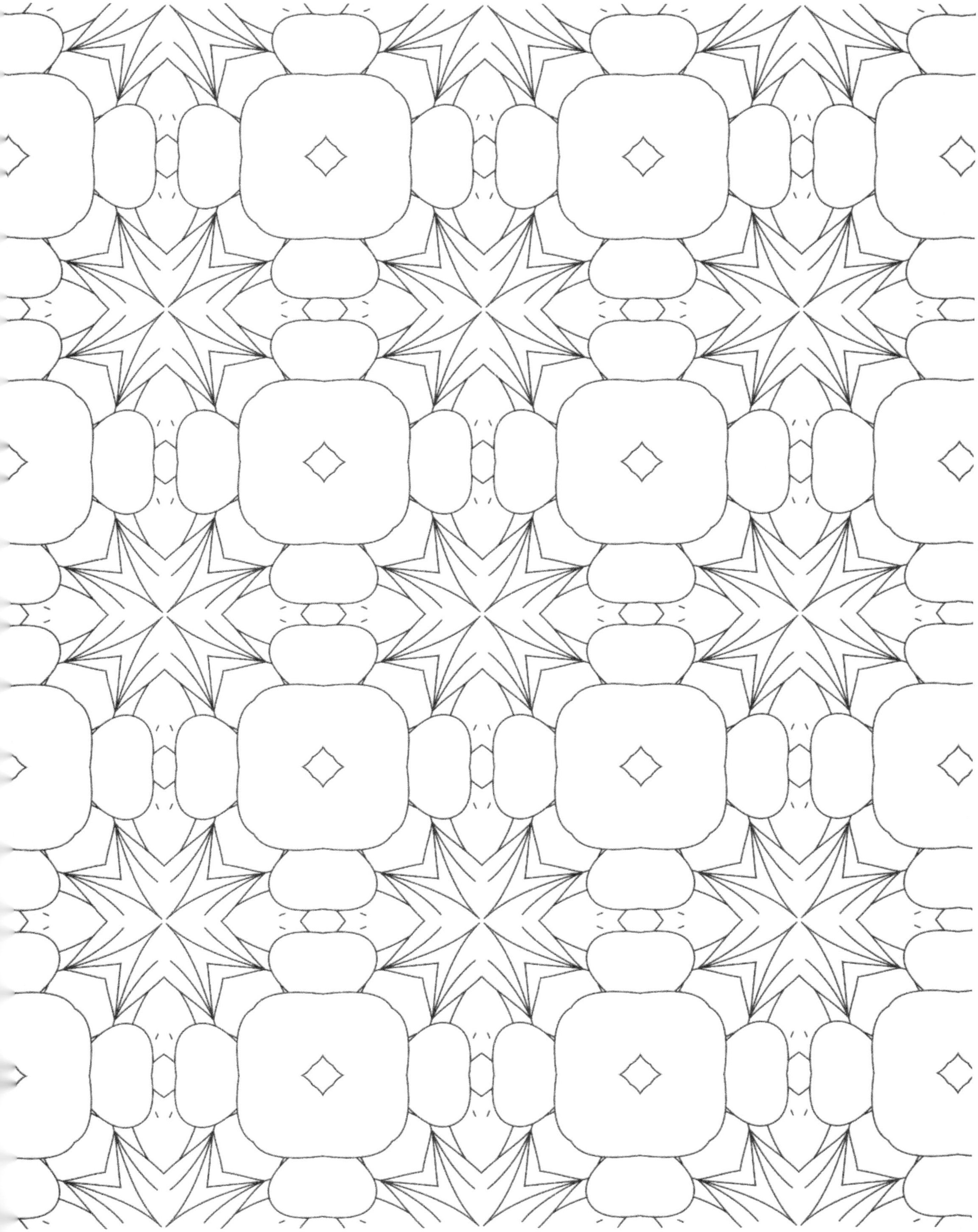

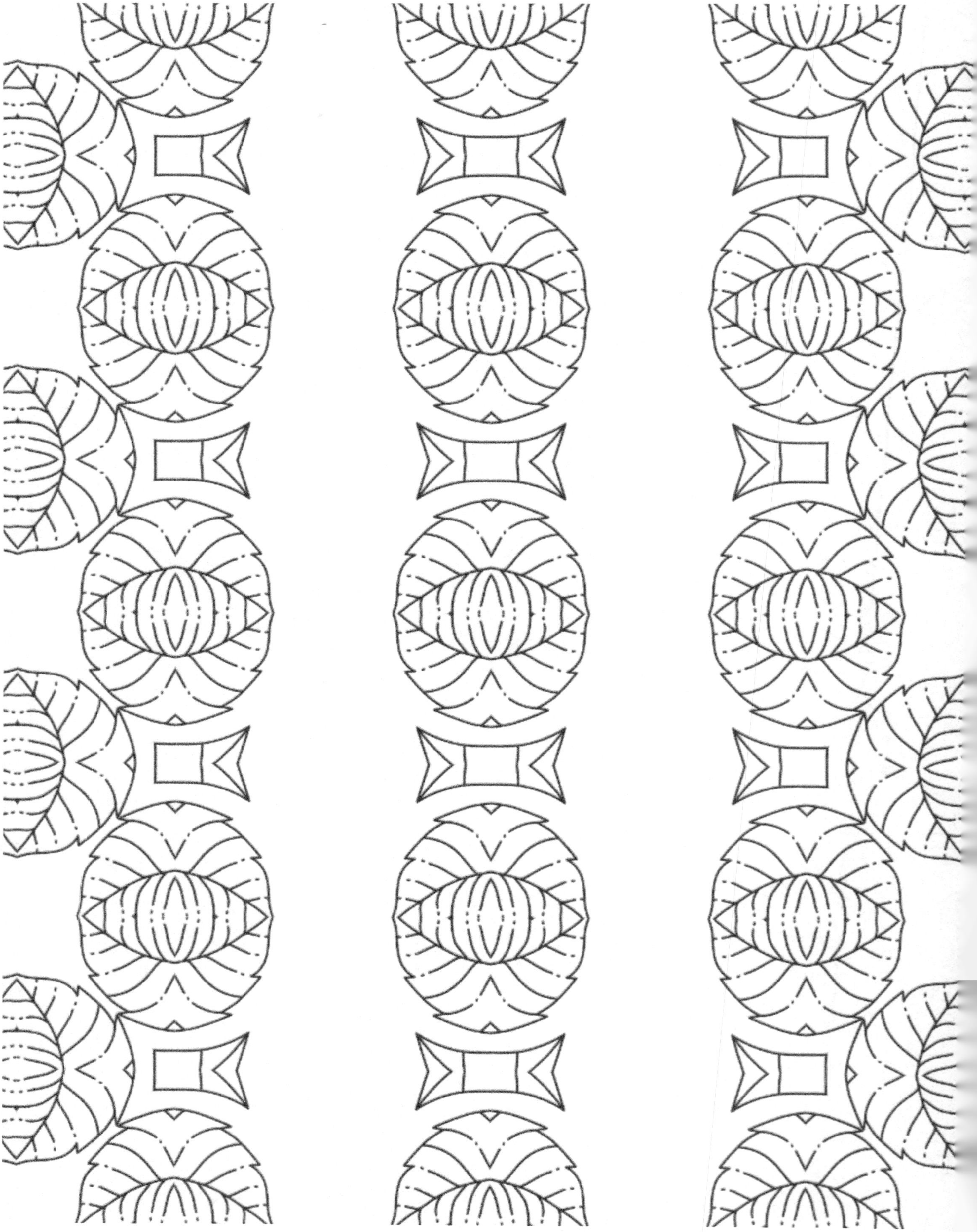

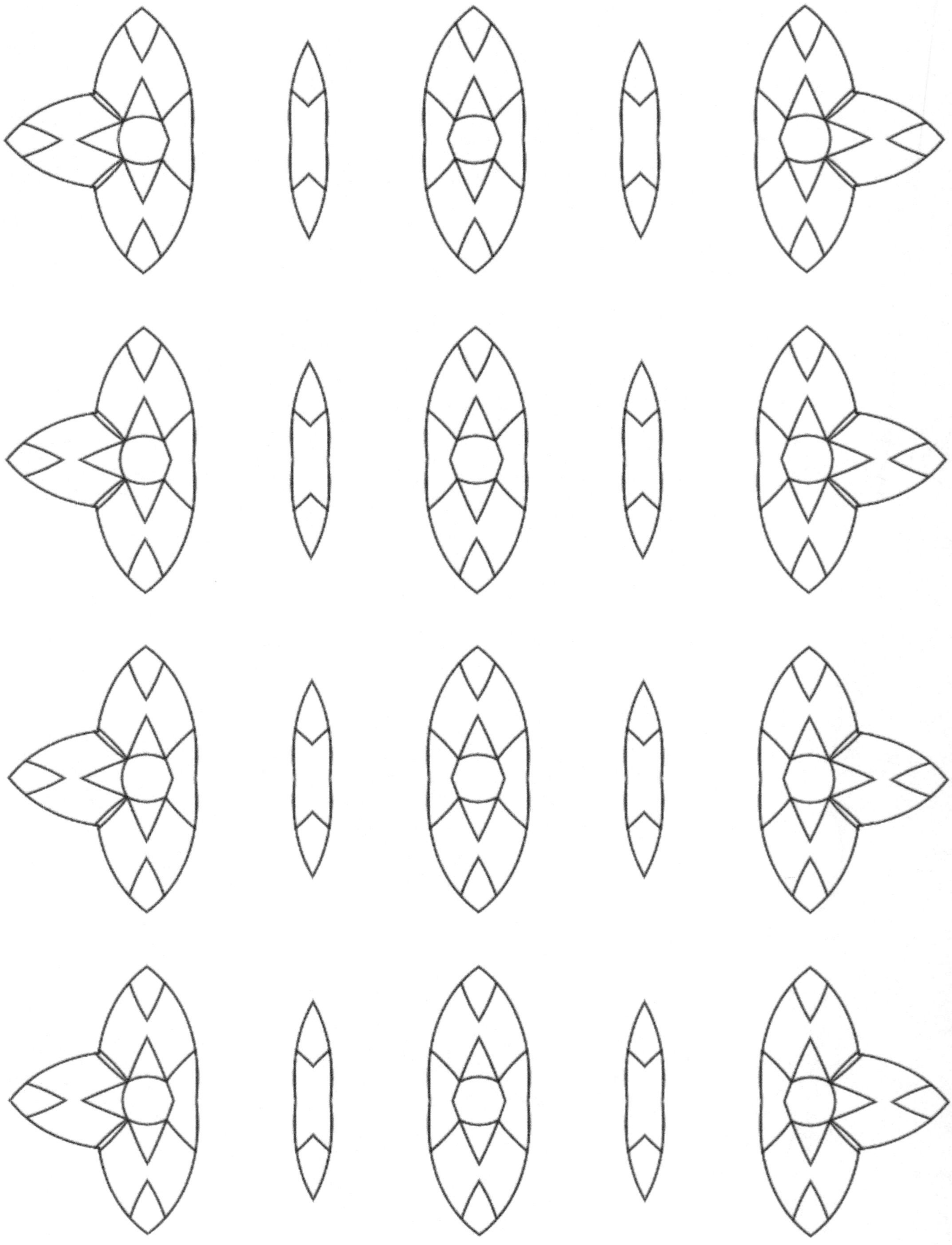

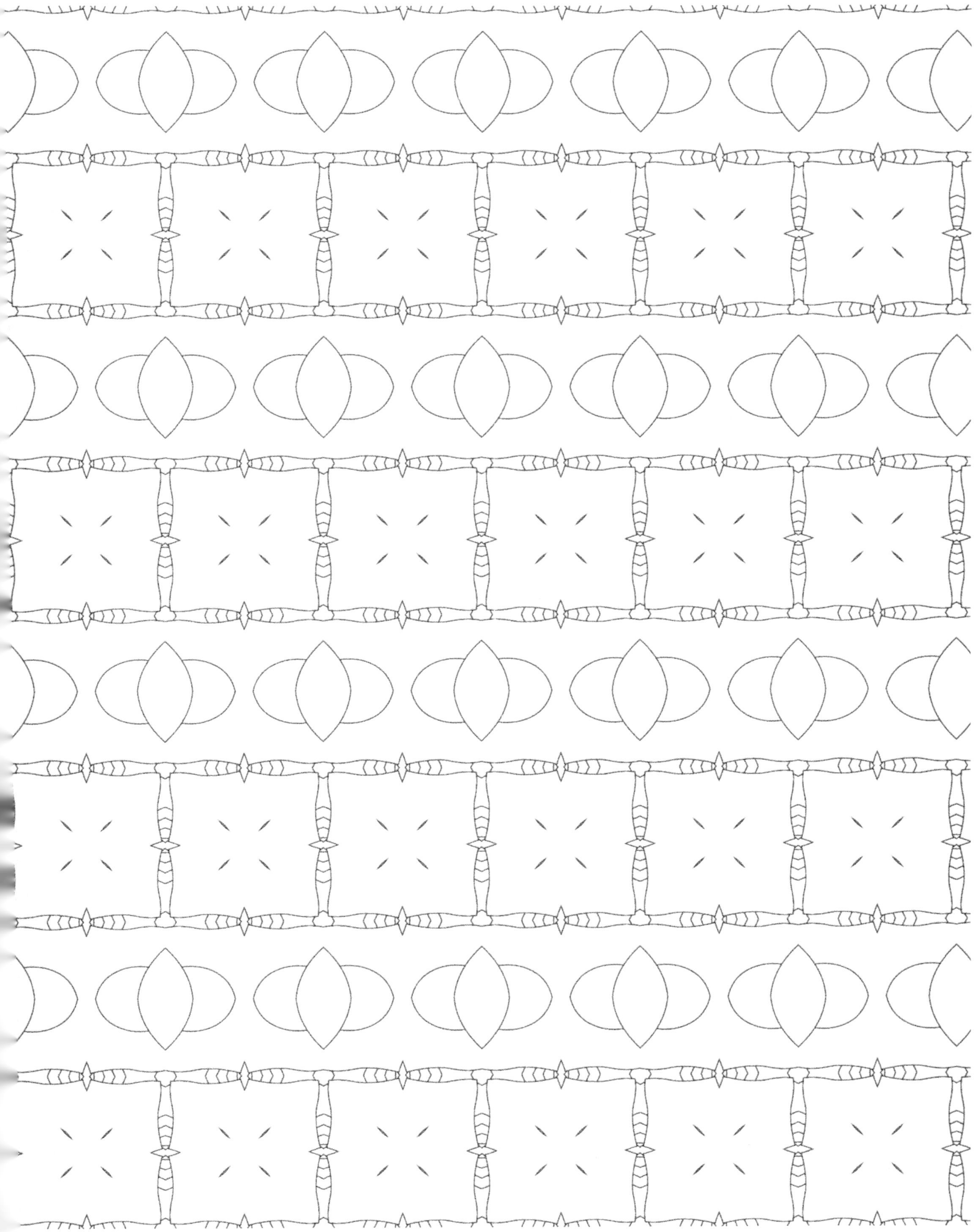

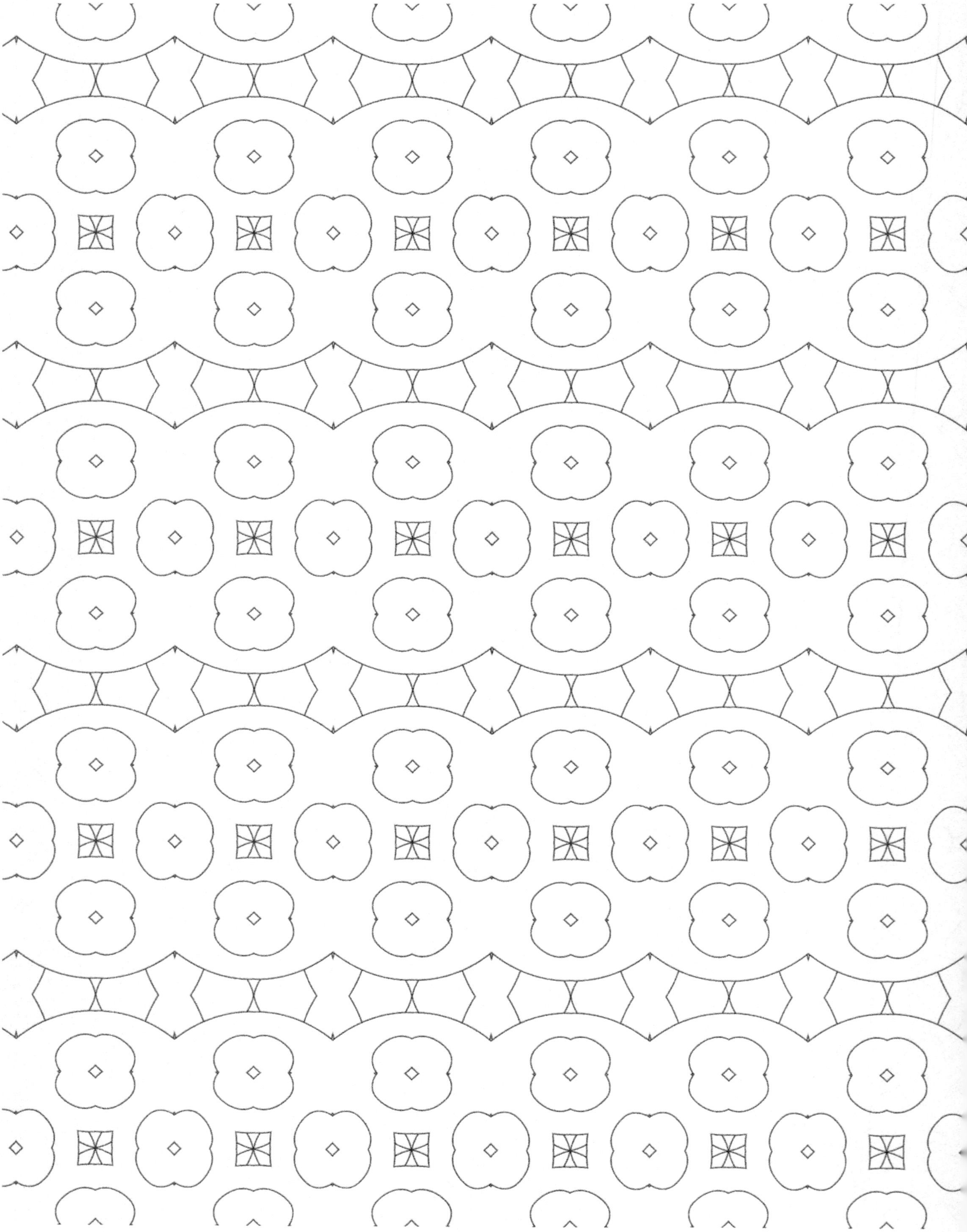

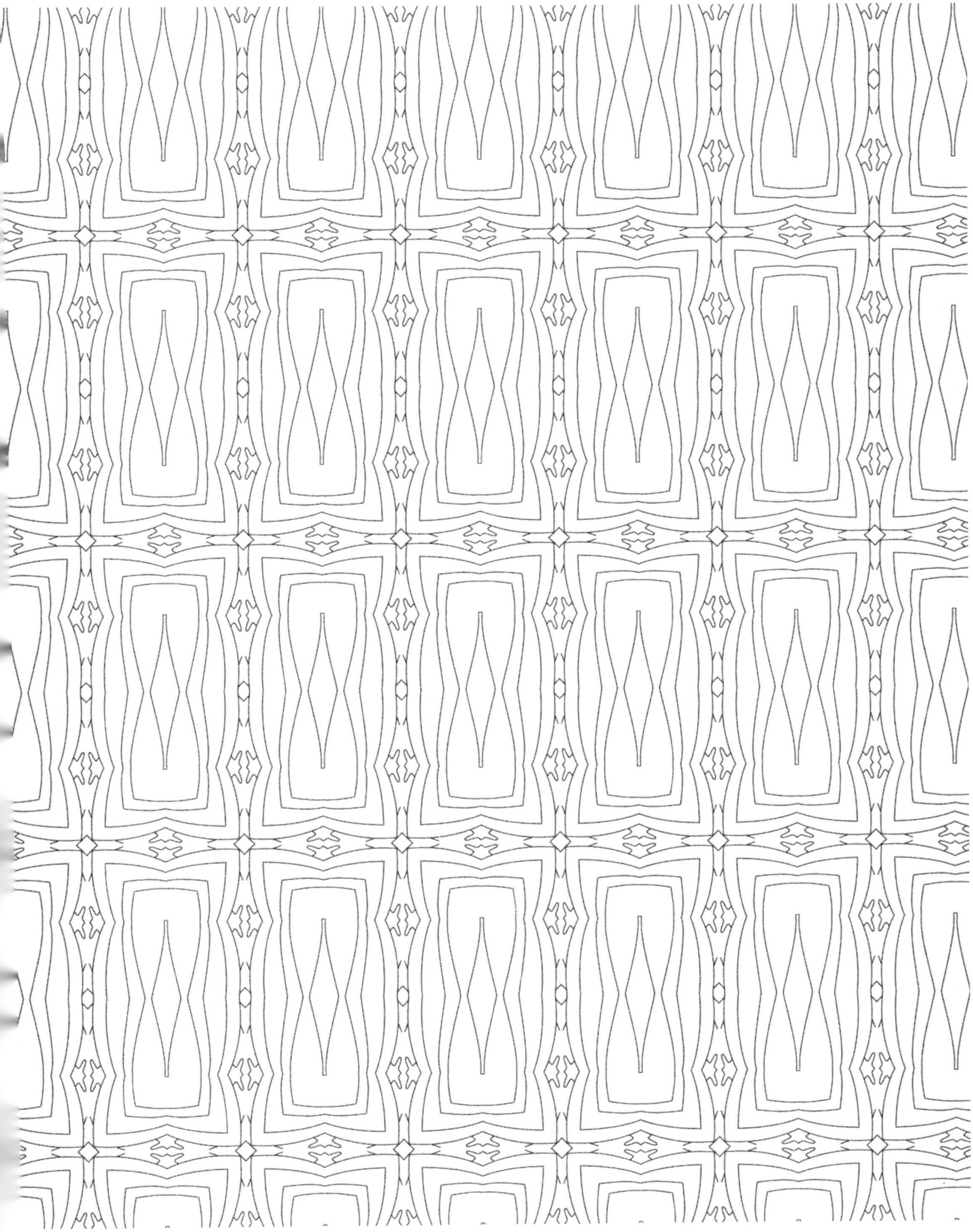

Made in the USA
Monee, IL
29 August 2023

41813203R10111